A Sea Star

Written by Anne Miranda

This is a sea star.

It was born in the sea.

It was found at the shore.

This sea star has five arms.

Some sea stars have more.

A sea star has many tube feet.

It can't go very far.

But it can hold onto a rock in a storm.

It is hard to open a clam shell.

But a sea star can open a clam shell.

It eats the clam.

This part is its mouth.

Come see sea stars any time.